Wars Waged Under the Microscope

The War Against Malaria

Cynthia O'Brien

CRABTREE
PUBLISHING COMPANY
WWW.CRABTREEBOOKS.COM

CRABTREE
PUBLISHING COMPANY
WWW.CRABTREEBOOKS.COM

Author: Cynthia O'Brien

Editors: Sarah Eason, Jennifer Sanderson, and Ellen Rodger

Editorial director: Kathy Middleton

Design: Simon Borrough

Cover design and additional artwork: Katherine Berti

Photo research: Rachel Blount

Proofreader: Wendy Scavuzzo

Production coordinator and Prepress technician: Ken Wright

Print coordinator: Katherine Berti

Consultant: David Hawksett

Produced for Crabtree Publishing by Calcium Creative Ltd

Photo Credits

Cover: tl: Brian Ongoro, Shutterstock; All other images Shutterstock

Inside: Flickr: US President's Malaria Initiative: pp. 26, 29; Nothingbutnets.net: @Georgina Goodwin/UNF: p. 20; Shutterstock: 3d man: p. 10; Abugrafie: p. 25; Scisetti Alfio: p. 19; Anton Ivanov: p. 6; Avatar 023: p. 4; Somboon Bunproy: p. 12; Christoph Burgstedt: p. 15; Kateryna Kon: p. 14; Mama Belle and the kids: p. 13; Riccardo Mayer: p. 23; Jaroslav Moravcik: p. 9; Brian Ongoro: p. 17; PongMoji: p. 21; PPK Studio: p. 22; Yurchanka Siarhei: p. 11; Schira: p. 8; Tayvay: p. 7; Tonhom1009: pp. 16, 24 & 28; Oleg Znamenskiy: p. 5; Wikimedia Commons: Joana Rosario/President's Malaria Initiative: p. 18; US AID/Liberia: p. 27

Library and Archives Canada Cataloguing in Publication

Title: The war against malaria / Cynthia O'Brien.
Names: O'Brien, Cynthia (Cynthia J.), author.
Description: Series statement: Wars waged under the microscope | Includes bibliographical references and index.
Identifiers: Canadiana (print) 2021018907X | Canadiana (ebook) 20210189088 | ISBN 9781427151308 (hardcover) | ISBN 9781427151384 (softcover) | ISBN 9781427151469 (HTML) | ISBN 9781427151544 (EPUB)
Subjects: LCSH: Malaria—Juvenile literature. | LCSH: Malaria—Treatment—Juvenile literature. | LCSH: Malaria—Prevention—Juvenile literature. | LCSH: Epidemics—Juvenile literature.
Classification: LCC RC157 .O27 2022 | DDC j614.5/32—dc23

Library of Congress Cataloging-in-Publication Data

Names: O'Brien, Cynthia (Cynthia J.) author.
Title: The war against malaria / Cynthia O'Brien.
Description: New York, NY : Crabtree Publishing Company, [2022] | Series: Wars waged under the microscope | Includes index.
Identifiers: LCCN 2021016679 (print) | LCCN 2021016680 (ebook) | ISBN 9781427151308 (hardcover) | ISBN 9781427151384 (paperback) | ISBN 9781427151469 (ebook) | ISBN 9781427151544 (epub)
Subjects: LCSH: Malaria--Juvenile literature. | Malaria--Treatment--Juvenile literature. | Malaria--Prevention--Juvenile literature. | Epidemics--Juvenile literature.
Classification: LCC RC157 .O27 2022 (print) | LCC RC157 (ebook) | DDC 614.5/32--dc23
LC record available at https://lccn.loc.gov/2021016679
LC ebook record available at https://lccn.loc.gov/2021016680

Crabtree Publishing Company
www.crabtreebooks.com   1-800-387-7650

Printed in the U.S.A./062021/CG20210401

Published in Canada
Crabtree Publishing
616 Welland Ave.
St. Catharines, Ontario
L2M 5V6

Published in the United States
Crabtree Publishing
347 Fifth Ave.
Suite 1402-145
New York, NY 10016

Contents

The Enemy

People have been battling malaria for many thousands of years, and the fight continues today. Malaria is a serious, sometimes deadly, disease caused by a **pathogen**. In 2019, there were about 229 million cases of malaria around the world. In the same year, 409,000 people died of the disease.

What Causes Malaria?

The pathogen that causes malaria is a **parasite**. Certain species, or types, of the female *Anopheles* mosquito pick up the parasite from people who have it. The mosquitoes then bite other people and pass on the parasite. Children under five years old and pregnant women are most at risk. Other people at risk are the elderly and people who have traveled from countries with no malaria to countries where malaria is a problem. All these people have little **immunity**, or natural protection, against the disease and therefore easily get sick.

Dealing with Malaria

All people who travel to or live in places where malaria is a problem are encouraged to protect themselves by covering their skin with clothing and by sleeping under a **mosquito net**. There are also treatments for the disease.

It is especially important that children under the age of five have access to doctors who can provide medicine to help prevent malaria, as well as treat children who have it.

The Problem with Malaria

Although malaria can be prevented, treated, and cured, it is a difficult disease to control. This is mainly due to where it occurs. Most cases are in African countries south of the Sahara Desert, but malaria is also a problem in Eastern Europe, Southeast Asia, and Central and South America. Mosquitoes thrive in these places, and many people there are poor and do not have access to mosquito nets or medical treatment. This makes tackling the disease very difficult.

Travelers sometimes return home with the disease when they visit countries where malaria still exists. Every year, about 2,000 Americans return to the United States with malaria and must be treated.

"...we're dealing with a really complex enemy...this enemy takes place often in the hardest-to-reach areas, affecting **impoverished communities** with little access to health systems...We have very imperfect tools. So all of this put together means we're fighting what some have termed the biggest enemy of mankind in history."

Dr. Pedro Alonso, Director of the Global Malaria Programme, World Health Organization (WHO)

Malaria Hotspot

African countries have more than 90 percent of the world's malaria cases. For the people living in Africa, malaria is a constant threat. In 2019, more than 274,000 African children died from the disease.

The Right Conditions

Today, in countries south of the Sahara Desert, species of *Anopheles* mosquito carry a complicated parasite that causes more serious cases of malaria. The **climate** and **environment** in these hot African countries is ideal for mosquitoes. Rainy seasons bring flooding, which creates stagnant, or standing, water. The mosquitoes lay 50 to 200 eggs at a time. The mosquitoes then bite people and lay more eggs, causing a cycle that is impossible to break.

Malaria is dangerous for pregnant women and their unborn children.

CASE STUDY: LIVING IN A MALARIA ZONE

Nigeria has about one-quarter of the world's malaria cases. More than half of Nigerians live in poverty and in **remote** areas. Many people do not have money to buy mosquito nets to sleep under or **insecticides**. Hospitals and clinics are usually far away from these **rural** communities, and many do not have access to transportation if they need to get to a hospital.

Nigerians spend a lot money on preventing and treating malaria. This leaves them with less for food and other supplies. When they are sick, the treatment costs money. Being sick also means that they cannot work and earn the money. When children become sick, they cannot help their parents on their farms and they cannot go to school.

Global organizations and charities are trying to change things for the better. This involves health care workers who teach people how to prevent malaria and how to treat it. It means getting mosquito nets to people, setting up clinics in remote areas, and making sure people get the right medication.

Every two minutes, a child dies of malaria somewhere in the world. Many are in Africa. Better medication will help stop this from happening.

The Battle Begins

Malaria has been attacking people for thousands of years. Ancient Indian writings from as far back as 1500 BCE called it the "king of diseases." Malaria was a problem for the ancient Chinese, Greeks, and Romans, too. But it took many centuries for people to understand what caused this terrible illness.

The First Breakthroughs

People believed that malaria came from swamps and traveled through the air. In the early 1800s, they began using the name "malaria." It comes from the Italian words for "bad air." However, in the later 1800s, the true cause of this disease was revealed. While working in North Africa in 1878, a French military doctor named Alphonse Laveran examined blood **samples** from malaria patients. He did many tests and discovered that there was something invading the patients' **red blood cells**. In 1880, Laveran identified the **protozoan** parasite that causes the disease. He and another scientist named Patrick Manson also suggested that mosquitoes might carry the parasite.

Laveran studied the malaria parasite at its different stages. Here, the ring shapes are the parasite in its growing stage in the blood.

Identifying the Mosquito

In 1895, British doctor Sir Ronald Ross began studying malaria. He wanted to find out if Laveran and Manson were right about mosquitoes carrying the parasite. Ross was living in India, where mosquitoes were common. Meanwhile, a group of Italian scientists was working on the same ideas. In 1897, Ross and the Italians discovered that the parasite grew in the *Anopheles* mosquito and that the mosquito carried the parasite from person to person.

A Global Fight

Once scientists identified what caused malaria, they could fight it. Insecticides, drugs, and window screens helped eliminate, or get rid of, malaria in North America by the 1950s. Twenty years later, Europe had eliminated it, too. From 1998, the Roll Back Malaria Partnership brought together governments, organizations, and others to share information, raise money, and fight for a common cause: eradicating malaria everywhere.

In 2010, scientists discovered evidence of malaria parasites in the remains of the Egyptian pharaoh, or king, Tutankhamun. He ruled ancient Egypt more than 3,300 years ago.

An Invisible Threat

Microorganisms, or microbes, are everywhere, but the human eye cannot see them. They are tiny organisms, or living things, which are visible only under a microscope. This is a device that magnifies things, or makes them bigger. Microbiologists are scientists who study microbes so they can understand more about them. Some microbes are pathogens that cause disease.

Using microscopes, microbiologists can see pathogens, such as this protozoa, clearly. The microscopes can produce images that look three-dimensional (3-D), not flat.

Where Are Microbes Found?

Microbes are found in soil, water, plants, and even in the human body. In fact, the human body has more microbe **cells** than human cells. However, most microbes do not cause disease and many of these tiny organisms are actually helpful. For example, **bacteria** in the digestive system break down food to make **nutrients** the body can use. Different parts of the body contain different combinations of microbes, and each person has a unique **microbiome**. Pathogens may cause disease in one person but not in another.

Enemy Invaders

The main types of pathogen are **viruses**, bacteria, **fungi**, and protozoa. Often, other microbes can keep pathogens under control as part of the body's **immune system**. But if the pathogens invade the body and multiply, they can cause illnesses such as colds, measles, and malaria.

Pathogens enter the body in different ways. People may eat food **contaminated** with bacteria. People also pass infections to each other directly, for example, by sneezing on them and passing on a cold virus. Humans can pick up infections from surfaces, then touch their eyes, nose, or face, which lets the pathogen into the body. Some pathogens, including the malaria parasite, rely on insects or other animals to transmit them, or pass them on.

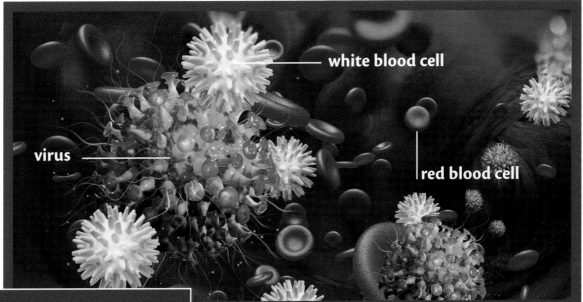

white blood cell

virus

red blood cell

White blood cells *move through the body's blood and* ***tissue****. They destroy invading microbes and remove dead cells. Special white blood cells also produce* ***proteins*** *called* ***antibodies*** *that attack pathogens.*

UNDER THE MICROSCOPE

The body's immune system goes to war against pathogens right away. The first defense is the skin, which keeps out most pathogens. If pathogens get inside the body, white blood cells attack them. Some signs, or symptoms, of illness show that the immune system is doing its job. For example, a **fever** can help the immune system work better.

Under Attack

The malaria parasite relies on female mosquitoes and humans to survive. The female mosquito bites people to get the blood it needs for protein to produce eggs. If a person already has the malaria parasite in their blood, the mosquito takes in the parasite with the blood.

Parasite Invasion

The parasite does not hurt the mosquito. Instead, it **reproduces** inside the mosquito. Then, when the mosquito bites other people, it injects the parasites into them through its saliva, or spit. Once inside the human body, the parasite starts its attack in the liver. The parasite multiplies and goes on to invade the body's red blood cells. The parasite invaders grow inside healthy blood cells and destroy them.

About 70 different species of Anopheles mosquitos carry malaria parasites.

The Symptoms

It can take just seven days or up to an entire month for people to develop malaria symptoms. It depends on the type of malaria parasite and the person's own immune system as to what symptoms the person will show. Sometimes, symptoms are mild, such as feeling weak and having a slight fever. More often, people with malaria have fever, headaches, sweats, **nausea**, and muscle aches. Malaria can become much worse in a short period of time, so it is crucial for people to seek treatment right away. Malaria can lead to **anemia,** as well as breathing problems, brain injury, and death. However, unlike some diseases, malaria is not contagious, or spread from person to person.

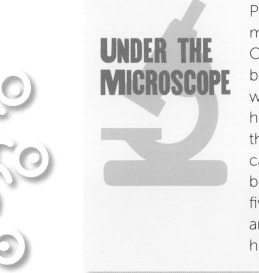

If someone has malaria, they may need medicine that can go directly into their bloodstream. This may mean a stay in the hospital on a medicine drip.

UNDER THE MICROSCOPE

People never develop full immunity to malaria. This means they can be reinfected. Often, the next infections are not as bad, because the body created some antibodies with the first infection. These antibodies help the body's immune system fight the parasite a little better. But, antibodies can disappear over time and people can become very sick again. Children under five years have not had time to develop any antibodies, so that is why they are at high risk of getting the disease.

A Tiny Enemy

Different species of mosquitos can infect humans with other diseases. A bite from an infected mosquito can cause diseases such as yellow fever, West Nile virus, and Zika virus. The *Anopheles* mosquito carries one of five different parasites that cause malaria in humans. Two of them can cause serious harm and death.

Malaria Up Close

The malaria parasite is a single-celled protozoan microbe. Although there are five types that infect humans, the *Plasmodium falciparum* and *Plasmodium vivax* parasites are the most dangerous. In Africa, the *Plasmodium falciparum* parasite causes almost all cases of malaria. *Plasmodium vivax* is common in Central and South America and Asia. The different parasites behave in different ways. The *Plasmodium ovale* malaria parasite may not cause serious illness, but it can stay in the liver for many months. If that happens, it can cause symptoms to reappear long after the first infection.

After breaking out of the liver cells, the parasite invades red blood cells in a ring-shaped form called a trophozoite.

Plasmodium falciparum is the most dangerous of all malaria parasites because it multiplies more quickly in the blood. It is also the parasite that can cause cerebral malaria, which is an infection in the brain.

The Parasite at Work

The malaria parasite goes through different stages inside the mosquito and after it invades the human body. It enters the body in the form of **sporozoites**, which can reach the liver in 30 minutes. Once there, the sporozoites start changing and producing many thousands of attacking **antigens**. These antigens infect the red blood cells until they burst. This allows them to spread out, attack more cells, and change again.

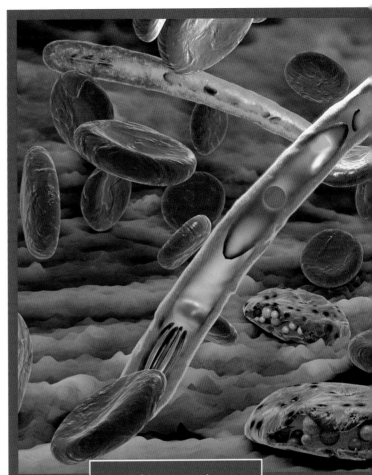

Long, thin sporozoites head straight for liver cells, which the parasite uses to change into merozoites. These are the antigens that attack red blood cells.

UNDER THE MICROSCOPE

Microbiologists diagnose malaria by looking at patients' blood samples under a microscope. They put a smear of blood on a glass slide, then the blood is stained with a dye so they can see the parasites more clearly. Scientists also look at the samples to identify and study the malaria parasite to help them find the right medicines for each patient.

Studying the Enemy

Scientists around the world are fighting against malaria by using their skills in the lab. They study the way the parasite behaves, how it adapts and changes, and different ways to stop it from infecting people.

In the Field and the Lab

Many pathogens, including the malaria parasite, exist in nature. Microbiologists studying the *Anopheles* mosquito often work in the field. This means they can study wild, live bugs that have not adapted to, or changed to cope with, a laboratory setting. The studies help scientists understand many things, from how the parasite develops in mosquitoes to how it survives.

Scientists use microscopes to identify the Anopheles mosquito and to study how the parasite behaves inside the mosquito.

A microbiology lab has specialized tools, including state-of-the-art microscopes. Other equipment helps analyze cells or helps to grow malaria parasites to study them. Scientists test millions of substances to see how they react with the malaria parasite. They keep detailed records of all of their investigations and results. They publish, or make public, their reports to share their findings with other scientists.

CASE STUDY: MICROBIOLOGISTS AT THE CUTTING EDGE

Since 2014, scientists have been studying mosquitoes that live around Lake Victoria, in Kenya, East Africa. Although there are many *Anopheles* mosquitoes living in the area, there are fewer cases of malaria there than in other parts of the country. What is stopping these mosquitoes from transmitting the malaria parasite?

Scientists **breed** mosquitoes and test insecticides on them to see if the insecticides are effective.

At the beginning of their study, the scientists looked for bacteria. In 2014, a trial in Townsville, Australia, had shown that mosquitoes infected with a particular bacterium did not spread dengue fever, which is a serious disease. Instead, they found something quite different—just like in the Kenyan mosquitoes.

The team collected as many live mosquitoes as they could and took them to the nearby lab to study. They discovered that Microsporidia MB, which are microbes related to fungi, were living in the mosquitoes. The mosquitoes were not infected with the *Plasmodium* parasite because this other microbe was protecting them. This is an amazing find, but the research does not stop here. The next step is to figure out how to spread this microbe across a wider mosquito population. By doing that, the malaria parasite would not infect the mosquitoes, so the mosquitoes would not infect humans. It could be a major tool in eradicating, or completely getting rid of, malaria.

Armed with Medicine

For a long time, there were no drugs to treat a person with malaria. Some patients survived the illness, but many died. People caught malaria more than once. Modern medicine has developed new treatments, but this work is ongoing.

First Treatments

One of the first treatments for malaria came from the bark of the cinchona tree in Peru. In the 1600s, the Spanish took the bark back to Europe. Malaria patients took a powdered form of the bark to relieve many symptoms. In the 1920s, French scientists discovered that quinine was the important ingredient in the bark. Quinine became the main treatment for malaria. Quinine helps stop the parasites from reproducing, but it does not always kill them, so scientists needed to develop better drugs.

Community health care workers help distribute drugs to fight malaria. Patients must take these medicines over a few days to cure the infection.

Modern Treatments

After **World War II**, chloroquine became a leading **antimalarial drug**. However, the malaria parasite can develop **resistance** to medicines, so the more a certain drug is used, the more the parasite seems to adapt. For this reason, chloroquine had become less effective in some areas by the 1970s. However, it is still used to prevent and treat many cases of malaria.

By 2016, new drugs called artemisinin-based combination therapies (ACTs) had become the first choice for treating malaria. ACTs use a combination of ingredients that can kill parasites within three days. Doctors assess patients according to the type and number of parasites found in their blood, then decide on the right ACT to treat them. Severe cases need longer treatments.

The main ingredient of ACT medication is artemisinin, taken from the sweet wormwood plant. More than 2,000 years ago, the ancient Chinese used artemisinin to treat fevers.

"This particular parasite is very adaptable. Even if you kill it in the human bloodstream, it can move into the mosquito stage. Over time, it has adapted to survive...which is why it is difficult to control the disease."

Professor Rita Tewari, Professor of Parasite Cell Biology, University of Nottingham, United Kingdom (UK)

Taking It to the Front Line

Malaria can be prevented and it can be treated but, often, the people who need treatment live far from hospitals. They may have to walk for many hours to get help or may be too weak to travel. Like wartime soldiers, people who are fighting the battle against malaria need to bring help to tackle it in the worst-affected places.

Organizations such as Nothing But Nets help get mosquito nets to people, even in remote areas.

Stopping the Enemy

One of the most important battles against malaria is prevention, or stopping it from happening in the first place. If people do not get infected, they will not become sick and will not need treatment. Mosquitoes are most active at night, so people are at high risk while they are sleeping. One way to stop mosquitoes from biting is to make sure that, over their beds, people put up nets with small mesh that mosquitoes cannot fly through. The nets are treated with insecticide. This provides another layer of protection against mosquitoes.

Powerful Insecticide

During World War II, the military began using the insecticide dichlorodiphenyl-trichloroethane (DDT) to control malaria. However, DDT can be toxic, or poisonous. The United States and Canada banned it in 1972, but other countries continued to use it. Even so, mosquitoes developed a resistance to DDT. For example, in Sri Lanka, using DDT helped rid the country of malaria in the 1940s. Twenty years later, the mosquitoes were back and so was the disease. Other insecticides have replaced DDT, but scientists must watch to see if they remain effective.

Using insecticides kills mosquitoes, but they also kill other insects such as bees. It is not a good solution to stop the disease.

In the Community

Most antimalarial drugs are not made in countries where malaria is common. Drugs and other supplies used in the fight against malaria must be imported, or bought in. That is expensive and takes a long time. Making antimalarial drugs available for everyone is a vital weapon in the war against malaria.

At local clinics, rapid diagnostic tests (RDTs) can be life-saving tools. These tests give results in 15 to 30 minutes. However, they do not always detect the malaria parasite, especially if there are low numbers of them in the patient's blood. Sometimes, it is necessary to follow up with another, more accurate, test in a lab.

Searching for a Vaccine

Scientists have been researching malaria vaccines since the 1930s, but it was not until 1987 that scientists developed a vaccine that looked promising.

Shape-Shifting Parasites

The malaria parasite changes its form during its life cycle. There are also different types of malaria parasites. This makes developing a vaccine very difficult, because vaccines have to target the specific type of parasite at a certain stage. The vaccine developed in 1987 fights *Plasmodium falciparum*. It triggers the immune system to attack the parasite when it enters the body. However, it has to work quickly because the microbes travel to the liver and multiply. When they leave the liver, they are in a different form, so this vaccine is ineffective.

New malaria vaccines may be based on malaria parasites taken from mosquito saliva glands.

Other vaccines are being developed. Some are designed to attack the parasite in the liver, before it invades red blood cells. As scientists continue to learn more about the malaria parasite, there is a better chance that they will create a vaccine to beat it for good.

CASE STUDY: VACCINE ON TRIAL

The RTS,S vaccine became the first vaccine to offer some hope of protection against malaria. In 2016, the WHO announced that the vaccine would be launched for use in parts of Africa. Many organizations came together to start a vaccine program in Africa. These included the manufacturer, local government agencies in Africa, and the WHO.

On April 23, 2019, Malawi became the first country to use the new vaccine. The vaccine was introduced to two other countries—Ghana and Kenya—later in the year. One year later, 275,000 children had been vaccinated over the three countries. The program is set to continue until 2023.

The RTS,S vaccine has helped reduce the number of severe malaria cases. However, it does not provide complete protection from the disease. In fact, children need four rounds, or doses, of the vaccine, but this only gives them about 30 percent protection from severe malaria for four years. Other protections, such as bed nets and spraying inside walls, must be used alongside the RTS,S vaccine.

The WHO hopes that about 720,000 children will receive the malaria vaccine during the program. The children will be checked for any signs of malaria or other health issues.

New Weapons

Since 2000, the world's war on malaria has saved about 7 million lives. It has also prevented more than 1 billion cases of the deadly disease. Today's scientists are using the latest technologies to track the spread of the disease and find even better ways to stop it for good.

Race Against Time

The malaria parasite can become resistant to drugs and insecticides. In Asia, some ACT treatments are not working as well as they have in the past. This has caused malaria cases to rise there.

Entomologists—scientists who study insects—are working with disease experts to breed mosquitoes that cannot bite.

Tracking Changes

Scientists have to monitor the changes in mosquitoes and keep working on new non-artemisinin combination drugs, or non-ACTs. Some of the new drugs in development attack the parasite at its different stages. This kind of attack makes it very difficult for the parasite to adapt and become resistant to the drug. New vaccines are also in the works.

Doctors and scientists are also looking closely at the immune systems of people in malaria zones. Studying and working with the body's natural defenses may help scientists create drugs that work better.

Harmless Mosquito

Another area of research is breeding harmless mosquitoes. In an experiment in West Africa, scientists have released 10,000 mosquitoes into the wild. These mosquitoes have been bred so the female mosquito is unable to carry eggs. Scientists are also breeding mosquitoes that cannot carry the parasite. In both cases, these new mosquitoes, which will breed with wild mosquitoes, will not be able to spread malaria to people.

Researchers are working on a phone app that will alert people that the Anopheles mosquito is nearby. The app would identify the mosquitoes by the buzzing sound they make with their wings. To make this possible, researchers have processed recordings from the lab and the wild.

Future Warfare

Today, the war against malaria continues. The parasite is complicated, and scientists are still working to understand it better. It will take the efforts of many people, from scientists and fundraisers to medical professionals and volunteers, to get rid of malaria by 2050.

World Malaria Day

On April 25 every year, people come together to share information and to raise money and awareness about malaria. The idea began in Africa in 2001, but became a worldwide event in 2008. The day is a reminder that malaria is still a major problem in many countries. In 2020, World Malaria Day's campaign message was "Zero malaria starts with me." This means, that to win the fight against malaria, the world needs people in communities to work together with researchers, doctors, and governments. Everyone can make a difference.

The president of the United States launched the Malaria Initiative in 2005. At that time, malaria was killing 1.2 million people each year. The program provides funding, training, supplies, and more.

> *"If we double down on ending malaria now, the world will...save millions of people from needlessly dying from mosquito bites."*
>
> **Martin Edlund, Malaria No More**

Raising Money

Charitable organizations, such as the Bill & Melinda Gates Foundation, help to fund amazing science discoveries. New, quick tests may diagnose malaria without having to take a blood sample. Charities also fund studies. For example, one study discovered a special malaria-blocking microbe in certain African mosquitoes, making them harmless to humans.

Marches that take place on World Malaria Day help spread awareness about malaria. People can also use social media and write letters to their governments to create awareness.

Timeline

Over the centuries, the diagnosis and treatment of malaria has changed enormously as scientists develop the technology to learn about this deadly enemy.

270 B.C.E. Chinese writings describe malaria symptoms.

1600s Cinchona bark is used as a treatment for malaria.

1820 Quinine is taken from cinchona bark.

1880 Alphonse Laveran identifies the malaria parasite.

1897 Ronald Ross discovers that the *Anopheles* mosquito carries the malaria parasite.

1934 Hans Andersag discovers the drug chloroquine.

1952 Malaria is eliminated from the United States.

1955 The WHO's Global Malaria Eradication campaign begins.

1958 Malaria in Ethiopia in Africa kills more than 150,000 people.

1976 William Trager and J.B. Jensen grow the malaria parasite to study for vaccine research and to help develop new drugs.

1992 First malaria vaccine, RTS,S, enters tests.

1996 Insecticide-treated bed nets are proven to reduce child deaths by 20 percent.

1998 Roll Back Malaria Partnership is launched by the WHO, United Nations Children's Fund (UNICEF), United Nations Development Programme (UNDP), and World Bank.

2000 106 countries are still reporting cases of malaria.

2001 ACT drugs become the first choice for malaria treatment, as recommended by the WHO.

2008 First World Malaria Day takes place on April 25.

2016 R21 vaccine starts trials; 91 countries report malaria.

2019 The Lancet Commission report sets out a plan to eradicate malaria by 2050.

Glossary

anemia Having fewer red blood cells than is healthy

antibodies Substances produced by the body that fight off invading bacteria and viruses

antigens Invaders in the body, such as viruses

antimalarial drug A medicine that helps the body fight malaria

bacteria A single-celled organism that can cause disease

breed To keep animals for the purpose of producing young animals with particular characteristics

cells The smallest units of a living thing that can survive on their own, carrying out a range of life processes

charitable Describes a person or group that helps other people

climate The usual weather in an area

contaminated Made dirty or infected

environment Everything living and nonliving in a particular area

fever A high body temperature

fungi Living things that grow and feed on other living things

immune system The organs and other parts of the body that work together to protect it from sickness

immunity A body's ability to stop a disease from affecting it

impoverished communities Groups of people who live in regions where there may be little access to food, water, jobs, education, health care, or transportation

insecticides Chemicals used to kill insects

microbiome The collection and combination of microbes in the body

mosquito net A net put up around a bed to prevent mosquito bites

nausea Feeling sick

nutrients Substances in food that the body needs to function

parasite An organism that lives in or on another living thing and gets food from it

pathogen An organism that causes disease or makes people sick

proteins The substances that do most of the work in cells

protozoan Relating to protozoa, which are single-celled organisms

red blood cells Cells that carry oxygen from the lungs to other parts of the body

remote Far away from major cities

reproduces Makes copies of itself

resistance The ability to not be affected by something

rural Not in a city or built-up area

samples Small amounts of something, such as blood, for testing

sporozoites Spore-like forms of a parasite when they invade the human body

tissue A group of cells of the same type, such as muscle cells, that perform a job together

vaccines Substances that help protect against certain diseases

viruses Microscopic organisms that can cause sickness

white blood cells Cells in the body that fight infection

World Health Organization (WHO) An organization that helps governments improve their health services

World War II The war fought from 1939 to 1945 in which the Allies (including Britain, the Soviet Union, and the United States) defeated the Axis powers (including Germany, Italy, and Japan)

Learning More

Find out more about malaria and how the war against this deadly disease is being won.

Books

Ciletti, Barbara. *Malaria Parasites* (Awful, Disgusting Parasites).
Black Rabbit Books, 2017.

Donaldson, Olivia. *Malaria* (Deadliest Diseases of All Time).
Cavendish Square, 2015.

Ford, Jeanne Marie. *Malaria: How a Parasite Changed History* (Infected!).
Capstone Press, 2019.

Hardyman, Robyn. *Fighting Malaria* (Tiny Battlefields).
Gareth Stevens, 2014.

Websites

Understand how pathogens work at:
www.dkfindout.com/us/human-body/body-defenses/germs-and-disease

For a simple overview of malaria, log on at:
www.kids.britannica.com/kids/article/malaria/394698

Find out more about mosquitoes, including the *Anopheles* mosquito, at:
https://kids.nationalgeographic.com/animals/invertebrates/facts/mosquito

See historical and modern photographs about malaria at:
www.nationalgeographic.com/science/health-and-human-body/human-diseases/malaria/#/1062.jpg

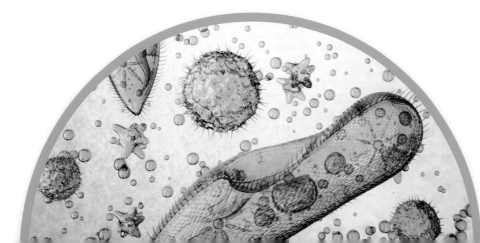

Index

ABOUT THE AUTHOR

Cynthia O'Brien has written many books for children, including books about science and how the body works. Researching this book, she learned a lot about malaria and the work that microbiologists and others are doing in the fight against it.